WE ARE THE
GOAL SCORERS
The Top Point Leaders of the NHL

WE ARE THE GOAL SCORERS

THE TOP POINT LEADERS OF THE NHL

NHLPA

CHRISTOPHER JORDAN

FENN
TUNDRA

INTRODUCTION

All NHL players share a passion
for hockey. From a young age, they
commit themselves to learning the
sport and bettering their skills. They
worked hard to become the very best.

The road to the NHL is a long one.
There are many young players chasing
a spot on a select team, looking to
be drafted—first in the bantam draft
and through the NHL Draft. But
being drafted doesn't always mean
an immediate spot on an NHL roster.
Many players need to first prove
their skills and commitment in the
minor leagues and work hard to earn
a chance to play in the NHL. Once
there, players have to show up to

every practice and every game with the right attitude and the determination to win. There will always be another player wanting that spot on the roster. Therefore NHL players can be considered the world's greatest hockey players. They are the players who, as young boys, led their junior teams, topped the minor leagues, and always played at the highest level of competition to show NHL scouts that they were ready for the big leagues. And they continue to play hard night after night, season after season.

We celebrate the game's very best in this book. These are the NHL's goal scorers.

SIDNEY CROSBY

PITTSBURGH PENGUINS

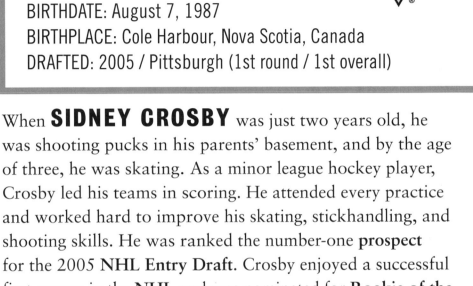

NUMBER: 87
POSITION: Center
SHOOTS: Left
HEIGHT: 5'11"
WEIGHT: 200 pounds
BIRTHDATE: August 7, 1987
BIRTHPLACE: Cole Harbour, Nova Scotia, Canada
DRAFTED: 2005 / Pittsburgh (1st round / 1st overall)

When **SIDNEY CROSBY** was just two years old, he was shooting pucks in his parents' basement, and by the age of three, he was skating. As a minor league hockey player, Crosby led his teams in scoring. He attended every practice and worked hard to improve his skating, stickhandling, and shooting skills. He was ranked the number-one **prospect** for the 2005 **NHL Entry Draft**. Crosby enjoyed a successful first season in the **NHL** and was nominated for **Rookie of the Year**. In his second **NHL** season, he led the league in scoring. He started his third season as the Penguins' captain. Crosby is a **Stanley Cup** champion and an Olympic gold medalist. His gold medal–winning goal in overtime at the 2010 Winter Olympics is one of the most talked-about goals in hockey history.

Crosby uses his amazing stickhandling skills to send long, straight **passes** to teammates to create scoring chances. He **sees the ice** better than most, and this allows him to move the puck up the ice and score often.

PAVEL DATSYUK

DETROIT RED WINGS

NUMBER: 13
POSITION: Center / Left wing
SHOOTS: Left
HEIGHT: 5'11"
WEIGHT: 198 pounds
BIRTHDATE: July 20, 1978
BIRTHPLACE: Yekaterinburg, Russia
DRAFTED: 1998 / Detroit (6th round / 171st overall)

PAVEL DATSYUK, a two-time **Stanley Cup** winner, has won the **Lady Byng Memorial Trophy** four times and the **Frank J. Selke Trophy** three times. He has played in three **NHL All-Star Games** and won an Olympic bronze for his native Russia in 2002. Datsyuk's awards say a lot about him. He is a strong defensive forward and one of the **NHL's** most sportsmanlike players.

Datsyuk is also a creative goal scorer, making him one of the game's best **two-way players**. He has great stickhandling skills that allow him to keep the puck on his stick as he races from one end of the rink to the other. He is masterful at raising the puck over the goalie to find the open corners of the net. Datsyuk loves to **deke** and will often make the goalie think he is planning to shoot for one side of the net, only to move the puck to his backhand and score.

JORDAN EBERLE

EDMONTON OILERS

NUMBER: 14
POSITION: Right wing
SHOOTS: Right
HEIGHT: 5'11"
WEIGHT: 184 pounds
BIRTHDATE: May 15, 1990
BIRTHPLACE: Regina, Saskatchewan, Canada
DRAFTED: 2008 / Edmonton (1st round / 22nd overall)

JORDAN EBERLE spent four seasons with the Regina Pats of the **WHL**, and in 2010 he was named the **CHL** Player of the Year as the most outstanding player of the top three junior leagues in Canada—the **WHL, QMJHL,** and **OHL**. He was committed to hockey but also to his studies, and in 2008 he won the Doc Seaman Trophy as the **WHL**'s top scholastic player. The Edmonton Oilers were impressed by Eberle's enthusiasm and love of hockey and used their first-round draft pick to select this skilled player.

Eberle has great **on-ice awareness** and plays with incredible energy on each and every shift. He has a tremendously hard and accurate **slap shot.** He is a quick-skating winger and an effective **playmaker.** He can make long **passes** and plays very well **along the boards** and in the corners. He is a consistent player and has a tremendous future in the **NHL.**

PATRIK ELIAS

NEW JERSEY DEVILS

NUMBER: 26
POSITION: Center / Left wing
SHOOTS: Left
HEIGHT: 6'1"
WEIGHT: 195 pounds
BIRTHDATE: April 13, 1976
BIRTHPLACE: Trebic, Czech Republic
DRAFTED: 1994 / New Jersey (2nd round / 51st overall)

PATRIK ELIAS has won the **Stanley Cup** twice with New Jersey. While playing for the Czech Republic, he won two bronze medals at the **IIHF World Championship** and a bronze medal at the 2006 Winter Olympics. At the end of the 2001 season, he and Joe Sakic shared the **NHL**'s best **plus/minus rating** with an incredible plus-45. Elias has enjoyed a long **NHL** career. He is a smart player who stays out of the penalty box.

Elias can play on the wing as well as center. He has great **puck control** and can move quickly along the boards. He is a talented **passer** who earns a lot of assists. He holds a number of New Jersey records, including the most **hat tricks**, career points, and game-winning goals. He has a good **work ethic** and plays with confidence. Elias is an important member of the Devils.

MARIAN GABORIK

COLUMBUS BLUE JACKETS

NUMBER: 10
POSITION: Right wing
SHOOTS: Left
HEIGHT: 6'1"
WEIGHT: 204 pounds
BIRTHDATE: February 14, 1982
BIRTHPLACE: Trencin, Slovakia
DRAFTED: 2000 / Minnesota (1st round / 3rd overall)

MARIAN GABORIK has represented Slovakia five times at the **IIHF World Championship** and twice at the Olympics. Gaborik won the fastest-skater contest at the 2003 **NHL All-Star Game.** That was several seasons ago, but he is still one of the fastest skaters in the **NHL** and currently holds Minnesota's record for most goals and points in a career. He has played in three **NHL All-Star Games** and was named the **MVP** of the 2012 game.

Gaborik is known as a point-a-game player. This means that he averages a goal or an assist for each game he plays. He is also a terrific **two-way player.** Gaborik is a solid forward who will also **back-check** hard and skate deep into his team's end to help on defense. He **sees the ice** well and has very good stickhandling skills. He plays with confidence and good discipline.

CLAUDE GIROUX

PHILADELPHIA FLYERS

NUMBER: 28
POSITION: Center / Right wing
SHOOTS: Right
HEIGHT: 5'11"
WEIGHT: 172 pounds
BIRTHDATE: January 12, 1988
BIRTHPLACE: Hearst, Ontario, Canada
DRAFTED: 2006 / Philadelphia (1st round / 22nd overall)

CLAUDE GIROUX has played in two **NHL All-Star Games** and competed for Canada at the 2008 **IIHF World Junior Championship**. Before his **NHL** debut, he was a sensation in the **QMJHL**. In 2008, he played an important role in his team winning the **QMJHL** championship and was awarded the **Guy Lafleur Trophy** as the **MVP** of the postseason. He was the Flyers' first-round draft pick in the 2006 NHL Entry Draft, and by 2010–11 he was the team's leading scorer.

Giroux may not be the biggest player on the ice, but he sure is fast! He not only creates scoring chances for his teammates but is also a skilled stickhandler, which helps him to score often. He reads the play well and plays consistently night after night.

MARIAN HOSSA

CHICAGO BLACKHAWKS

NUMBER: 81
POSITION: Right wing
SHOOTS: Left
HEIGHT: 6'1"
WEIGHT: 210 pounds
BIRTHDATE: January 12, 1979
BIRTHPLACE: Stara Lubovna, Slovakia
DRAFTED: 1997 / Ottawa (1st round / 12th overall)

MARIAN HOSSA played in the **Stanley Cup** championship series three seasons in a row. In 2008, he played for Pittsburgh, and his team lost to the Detroit Red Wings. He played for Detroit in 2009 and lost to his old team, the Pittsburgh Penguins. In 2010, he played with Chicago and finally won his first **Stanley Cup** when the Blackhawks beat Philadelphia. When Blackhawks captain Jonathan Toews accepted **the Cup** from the **NHL** commissioner, the first player he passed it to was Hossa. The 2006–07 season was his best so far. He racked up one hundred points playing for the Atlanta Thrashers. Hossa has played for the Slovakian national team an incredible sixteen times!

Hossa is a scrappy forward who battles hard for the puck and won't give it up easily once he has it. He will battle for loose pucks and is not afraid of getting bumped around. He plays his position well, and he has good confidence and strong leadership skills.

JAROME IGINLA

BOSTON BRUINS

NUMBER: 12
POSITION: Right wing
SHOOTS: Right
HEIGHT: 6'1"
WEIGHT: 210 pounds
BIRTHDATE: July 1, 1977
BIRTHPLACE: Edmonton, Alberta, Canada
DRAFTED: 1995 / Dallas (1st round / 11th overall)

JAROME IGINLA is the former captain of the Calgary Flames, where he holds a number of club records, including most goals and games played, and he is the team's all-time point leader. He has won the **Art Ross Trophy** and the **Lester B. Pearson Award**. He has two Olympic gold medals that he won when playing for Canada at the 2002 and 2010 Winter Olympics.

Before the 2013 NHL trade deadline, Iginla was traded to Pittsburgh. Iginla is a team leader who can do it all. He can score, he can assist, and he can defend. He is a very strong player and will not give up the puck easily. Iginla is a true **playmaker**. He **sees the ice** well and plays with fantastic effort on every shift. He has an amazingly hard **slap shot** and a quick **wrist shot**. Iginla is well respected and one of the **NHL**'s best all-around **two-way players**.

Jarome Iginla was traded to the Boston Bruins in July 2013.

ERIK KARLSSON

OTTAWA SENATORS

NUMBER: 65
POSITION: Defense
SHOOTS: Right
HEIGHT: 6'0"
WEIGHT: 180 pounds
BIRTHDATE: May 31, 1990
BIRTHPLACE: Landsbro, Sweden
DRAFTED: 2008 / Ottawa (1st round / 15th overall)

ERIK KARLSSON was ranked as one of the best junior hockey players in Europe. The Senators thought he would make a good fit for their team and chose him as their first pick in the 2008 **NHL Entry Draft**. He worked very hard at the Senators' **training camp** and made the **roster** to play, but his first month in the **NHL** was difficult, and he was sent to Ottawa's minor-league team. A month later, after practicing hard, he returned to the Senators' **lineup**, and this time he played at an elite **NHL** level and stayed with the team.

Karlsson is a force on the blue line and has a booming **slap shot**. He is a great **set-up man**, as his fifty-nine assists in the 2011–12 season show. He is on the ice for most **power plays** and helps on Ottawa's **special teams**. He is a fast skater and an exciting player to watch.

PHIL KESSEL

TORONTO MAPLE LEAFS

NUMBER: 81
POSITION: Right wing
SHOOTS: Right
HEIGHT: 6'0"
WEIGHT: 202 pounds
BIRTHDATE: October 2, 1987
BIRTHPLACE: Madison, Wisconsin, United States
DRAFTED: 2006 / Boston (1st round / 5th overall)

PHIL KESSEL was part of the U.S. National Team Development Program before playing a season at the University of Minnesota and becoming one of the top-ranked **prospects** going into the 2006 **NHL Entry Draft**. He was picked fifth by the Bruins and played three seasons in Boston. In 2009, he was **traded** to Toronto, where he is currently an **alternate captain** for the Maple Leafs. He played for the United States during the 2010 Winter Olympics and competed in both the 2010 and 2011 **NHL All-Star Games**. In 2012, Kessel was sixth in the **NHL** in points.

Kessel skates hard and fast, and he likes to position himself in front of his **opponents**' net to create scoring chances. He has a lightning-quick shot that he can release with great aim and power. He can also set up his teammates with exceptional straight **passing** skills.

ANZE KOPITAR

LOS ANGELES KINGS

NUMBER: 11
POSITION: Center
SHOOTS: Left
HEIGHT: 6'3"
WEIGHT: 225 pounds
BIRTHDATE: August 24, 1987
BIRTHPLACE: Jesenice, Slovenia
DRAFTED: 2005 / Los Angeles (1st round / 11th overall)

ANZE KOPITAR is the first Slovenian to play in the **NHL**. He is a skilled **centerman** and was an important part of Los Angeles's 2012 **Stanley Cup** championship. He is a remarkable **two-way player** who works hard to set up scoring chances for his team and stop scoring chances for his **opponents**. Kopitar has won a number of L.A. Kings team awards: Best Newcomer Award, Best Defensive Player Award, Most Popular Player Award, and team **MVP**. He has also led the Kings in scoring for five seasons in a row.

Kopitar had twenty points in the 2012 playoffs, and each point helped the Kings on their way to winning **the Cup**. He is a great skater who **passes** the puck well. He is a big player who can play a skilled and physical style of hockey and is very strong in his **opponents' slot**, but he can also use his fancy skating skills to avoid contact with his **opponents** when needed.

ILYA KOVALCHUK

NEW JERSEY DEVILS

NUMBER: 17
POSITION: Right wing / Left wing
SHOOTS: Right
HEIGHT: 6'3"
WEIGHT: 230 pounds
BIRTHDATE: April 15, 1983
BIRTHPLACE: Tver, Russia
DRAFTED: 2001 / Atlanta (1st round / 1st overall)

ILYA KOVALCHUK first played professional hockey in the Russian Vysshaya Liga (Superleague). The Atlanta Thrashers drafted him to play in the **NHL**. He played seven full seasons for Atlanta, plus part of an eighth. In his **rookie** year with the team, he scored fifty-one points and was a finalist for the **Calder Memorial Trophy**. In 2010, he was **traded** to New Jersey Devils and continues to be a big part of the team to this day.

Kovalchuk is a talented goal scorer. His **slap shot** seems as fast as a rocket, and he is known to score from anywhere inside the blue line. Kovalchuk is a very speedy skater, and he usually wins races for the puck. He is a big, strong player who uses his size to keep the puck away from defenders, and he is a great stickhandler who plays with a consistent and positive attitude.

JOFFREY LUPUL

TORONTO MAPLE LEAFS

NUMBER: 19
POSITION: Left wing / Right wing
SHOOTS: Right
HEIGHT: 6'1"
WEIGHT: 206 pounds
BIRTHDATE: September 23, 1983
BIRTHPLACE: Fort Saskatchewan, Alberta, Canada
DRAFTED: 2002 / Anaheim (1st round / 7th overall)

TORONTO MAPLE LEAFS ®

As a junior, **JOFFREY LUPUL** played for the Medicine Hat Tigers of the **WHL**. He scored at least thirty goals each season, and one year he put the puck in the net fifty-six times. Later, he became the first Anaheim Duck to score a **hat trick** in the playoffs and to score four goals in a playoff game, including the overtime winner. Lupul arrived in Toronto at the midpoint of the 2010–11 season in a multi-player **trade** with Anaheim. In his second season with the Leafs, Lupul played very well with linemate Phil Kessel and began racking up a lot of points. His impressive play earned him an invitation to the 2012 **NHL All-Star Game,** where he scored twice.

Lupul is a strong player who has good offensive instincts. He is very powerful **along the boards** and in the corners, and he will battle hard against his **opponents** to get and keep the puck. Lupul is a gifted **playmaker** who **sees the ice** well. He is a good skater with terrific acceleration and balance.

EVGENI MALKIN

PITTSBURGH PENGUINS

NUMBER: 71
POSITION: Center
SHOOTS: Left
HEIGHT: 6'3"
WEIGHT: 195 pounds
BIRTHDATE: July 31, 1986
BIRTHPLACE: Magnitogorsk, Russia
DRAFTED: 2004 / Pittsburgh (1st round / 2nd overall)

EVGENI MALKIN is the **assistant captain** of the Pittsburgh Penguins. This superstar hockey player was the Penguins' first-round draft pick in the 2004 **NHL Entry Draft.** He left Russia to play in the **NHL** at the start of the 2006–07 season. During his **rookie** year, Malkin scored thirty-three goals and fifty-two assists and won the **NHL's Rookie** of the Year award, the **Calder Memorial Trophy.** In 2009, the Penguins won the **Stanley Cup** and Malkin was awarded the **Conn Smythe Trophy** as the most valuable player of the playoffs.

Malkin is a talented **playmaker.** He has strong **puck control**, which allows him to move around defenders and score often. He has lightning fast acceleration and can unload a hard shot with great aim and power while skating. Malkin has made his mark on the **NHL** and won the **Art Ross Trophy** in 2009 and 2012. He also won the **Ted Lindsay Award** in 2012 and the **Hart Memorial Trophy** in 2012.

RICK NASH

NEW YORK RANGERS

NUMBER: 61
POSITION: Right wing / Left wing
SHOOTS: Left
HEIGHT: 6'4"
WEIGHT: 219 pounds
BIRTHDATE: June 16, 1984
BIRTHPLACE: Brampton, Ontario, Canada
DRAFTED: 2002 / Columbus (1st round / 1st overall)

RICK NASH played junior hockey for the London Knights of the **OHL**. In his first season, 2000–01, he scored thirty-one goals and was selected as the OHL Rookie of the Year. Columbus snapped up this big winger in 2002 and put him on their **roster** at the start of the next season. In his **rookie** year, Nash was a finalist for the **Calder Memorial Trophy**. In his second **NHL** season, he won the Maurice Richard Trophy for most goals scored in the regular season. He, Jarome Iginla, and Ilya Kovalchuk each scored forty-one times that season to share the honor. Nash has played in five **NHL All-Star Games** and has represented Canada at several international events.

Nash is a great on-ice leader. He inspires his team with a great **work ethic**. He is a big, strong winger and a solid skater. He has fantastic **puck control** and a wickedly hard shot. Nash is an all-around great player.

JAMES NEAL

PITTSBURGH PENGUINS

NUMBER: 18
POSITION: Right wing / Left wing
SHOOTS: Left
HEIGHT: 6'2"
WEIGHT: 208 pounds
BIRTHDATE: September 3, 1987
BIRTHPLACE: Whitby, Ontario, Canada
DRAFTED: 2005 / Dallas (2nd round / 33rd overall)

JAMES NEAL played junior hockey in the **OHL** for the Plymouth Whalers. He became eligible for the **NHL Entry Draft** after his second season in the **OHL** and was picked by the Dallas Stars, thirty-third overall. In his first **NHL** season with the Stars, Neal scored twenty-four goals, which is a Dallas record for most goals scored by a **rookie**. Before the 2011 **trade** deadline, Neal was **traded** to the Penguins.

The puck doesn't stay on the blade of Neal's stick for long! When a **pass** comes his way, he will often surprise the goalie and defense and fire a **one-timer** toward the net. This big winger has a very quick shot and can often find the net to score. He works hard **along the boards** and is a tough competitor in the corners. He is an excellent skater, and defenders have a very tough time moving him away from the area in front of their net.

ALEX OVECHKIN

WASHINGTON CAPITALS

NUMBER: 8
POSITION: Left wing
SHOOTS: Right
HEIGHT: 6'3"
WEIGHT: 230 pounds
BIRTHDATE: September 17, 1985
BIRTHPLACE: Moscow, Russia
DRAFTED: 2004 / Washington (1st round / 1st overall)

ALEX OVECHKIN played his first game in the Kontinental Hockey League during the 2001–02 season. By the time he was eligible for the **NHL,** he had become the most talked about junior player in the game. Selected number one overall by the Washington Capitals in the 2004 **NHL Entry Draft,** Ovechkin ended his first season with 106 points and was named the NHL **Rookie** of the Year. In just his third **NHL** season he led the league in scoring to earn the Maurice Richard Trophy as the leading goal scorer. That same season he also captured the **Art Ross Trophy, Lester B. Pearson Award** and **Hart Memorial Trophy.**

Ovechkin plays with great physical intensity and with incredible passion. He **sees the ice** well and has tremendous goal scoring instincts. He is a fast skater and can change directions with the puck with ease. He is a creative **playmaker** and has a wicked shot that he unloads often. Ovechkin is a very exciting player to watch.

ZACH PARISE

MINNESOTA WILD

NUMBER: 11
POSITION: Left wing
SHOOTS: Left
HEIGHT: 5'11"
WEIGHT: 195 pounds
BIRTHDATE: July 28, 1984
BIRTHPLACE: Minneapolis, Minnesota, United States
DRAFTED: 2003 / New Jersey (1st round / 17th overall)

ZACH PARISE played for Team USA at the 2010 Olympics and was named to the tournament all-star team. He was named the **MVP** of the 2004 **IIHF World Junior Championship**. In the summer of 2012, Parise, who had become the captain of the New Jersey Devils, signed as a free agent with the Minnesota Wild. He is originally from the state of Minnesota, so he looked forward to returning home. The news delighted fans of the Wild, as any team in the league would have been thrilled and excited to have this talented goal scorer join their club.

Parise is a very balanced skater with great acceleration. He is a talented **playmaker** and creates good scoring chances for his teammates. He is a versatile player and is often on the ice to help his team kill penalties. He also plays regularly on the **power play**. Parise has a very hard **slap shot**. He can take a **pass** well and fire the puck quickly. He has a great **work ethic** and never stops playing until the whistle blows.

DANIEL SEDIN

VANCOUVER CANUCKS

NUMBER: 22
POSITION: Left wing
SHOOTS: Left
HEIGHT: 6'1"
WEIGHT: 187 pounds
BIRTHDATE: September 26, 1980
BIRTHPLACE: Ornskoldsvik, Sweden
DRAFTED: 1999 / Vancouver (1st round / 2nd overall)

DANIEL SEDIN and his twin brother, Henrik, play incredibly well together. When on the same shift, each seems to always know where the other is, which helps them set up amazing scoring chances. Sedin has led the Canucks in scoring three times and was named the team **MVP** in 2011. The NHLPA presented him with the **Ted Lindsay Award** in 2011 as the **NHL**'s most outstanding player. He led the league in scoring that same year and won the **Art Ross Trophy**. At the 2006 Olympic Winter Games, Sedin represented his home country of Sweden and won a gold medal. He and Henrik were both named the Swedish Athlete of the Year in 2011.

Sedin is a remarkable **two-way player** who has amazing **puck control** and rushes up the ice with great speed and determination. He and Henrik are great ambassadors for the sport of hockey.

HENRIK SEDIN

VANCOUVER CANUCKS

NUMBER: 33
POSITION: Center
SHOOTS: Left
HEIGHT: 6'2"
WEIGHT: 188 pounds
BIRTHDATE: September 26, 1980
BIRTHPLACE: Ornskoldsvik, Sweden
DRAFTED: 1999 / Vancouver (1st round / 3rd overall)

HENRIK SEDIN plays for Vancouver with his twin brother, Daniel. The Canucks' general manager at the time, Brian Burke, was committed to landing both brothers at the 1999 **NHL Entry Draft**. To do it, he negotiated **trades** and swapped draft picks with other **NHL** clubs to ensure that the Canucks held the second and third picks overall. The twins joined the Canucks for the start of the 2000–01. Sedin is the Canucks' captain and an **Art Ross Trophy** winner, a **Hart Memorial Trophy** recipient, and an **NHL All-Star**. He won an Olympic gold medal when playing for Sweden at the 2006 Winter Games.

Sedin has led the Canucks in scoring four times. He sets up scoring chances and is very skilled at winning **face-offs**. He **passes** the puck quickly and makes long passes when needed. Sedin has strong defensive skills, reading the play well to break up an offensive rush, and he skates deep into his own end to help clear the puck.

TYLER SEGUIN

DALLAS STARS

NUMBER: 19
POSITION: Center
SHOOTS: Right
HEIGHT: 6'1"
WEIGHT: 182 pounds
BIRTHDATE: January 31, 1992
BIRTHPLACE: Brampton, Ontario, Canada
DRAFTED: 2010 / Boston (1st round / 2nd overall)

Many Canadian boys dream of playing in the **NHL**. They also dream of winning the Stanley Cup. And at just nineteen years of age, **TYLER SEGUIN** achieved both of these dreams. Seguin and Taylor Hall were ranked the best junior players available for the 2010 **NHL Entry Draft**. The Edmonton Oilers chose Hall first, and Boston picked Seguin second. A year later, Seguin was a **Stanley Cup** champion with the Bruins. He was Boston's point leader in 2012. In 2013 he was traded to the Dallas Stars.

Seguin is a great puck handler and is a gifted skater with great mobility and acceleration. He can **deke** well and has several great shots that he can use. He can send a hard, powerful **slap shot** toward his **opponents**' net, or a quick **wrist shot** to catch the goalie by surprise. Seguin plays with an amazing work ethic and won't stop until the whistle blows.

Tyler Seguin was traded to the Dallas Stars in July 2013.

TEEMU SELANNE

ANAHEIM DUCKS

NUMBER: 8
POSITION: Right wing
SHOOTS: Right
HEIGHT: 6'0"
WEIGHT: 196 pounds
BIRTHDATE: July 3, 1970
BIRTHPLACE: Helsinki, Finland
DRAFTED: 1988 / Winnipeg (1st round / 10th overall)

TEEMU SELANNE was drafted by the original Winnipeg Jets in the first round of the 1988 draft. After 19 seasons in the **NHL**, his records for goals (76) and points (132) as a **rookie** still stand. Selanne has won a **Stanley Cup** championship and has played in ten **NHL All-Star Games**. He has won a bronze and silver medal at the **IIHF World Championship** and three Olympic medals—two bronze and a silver—as a member of Finland's national team.

Selanne is a **veteran** player with good leadership skills and still has the speed that gave him his nickname, the Finnish Flash. He is a true goal scorer who can put the puck exactly where he wants. Selanne is also a gifted **playmaker** and a solid skater. He is one of the best players the game has ever seen, and he continues to impress his fans season after season.

JASON SPEZZA

OTTAWA SENATORS

NUMBER: 19
POSITION: Center
SHOOTS: Right
HEIGHT: 6'3"
WEIGHT: 216 pounds
BIRTHDATE: June 13, 1983
BIRTHPLACE: Toronto, Ontario, Canada
DRAFTED: 2001 / Ottawa (1st round / 2nd overall)

JASON SPEZZA was named the top **CHL prospect** going into the 2001 **NHL Entry Draft** and Ottawa snapped up this big **center** as a first-round draft pick. He worked hard playing for the Senators' farm team and made the Ottawa **roster** for the 2003–04 season, finishing the year with fifty-five points. In his second season with the Senators, he scored an amazing ninety points. He has played his entire **NHL** career with the Senators. Canadian-born, Spezza has represented his country at the 2000 and 2001 **IIHF World Junior Championship** and the **IIHF World Championship** in 2008, 2009, and 2011.

Spezza is a very creative hockey player who has a tremendous **slap shot**, skates hard, and passes the puck with great accuracy. Spezza is a strong team leader and a great role model for young hockey players. He even visits schools in the Ottawa area to help kids understand the importance of knowing how to spell!

STEVEN STAMKOS

TAMPA BAY LIGHTNING

NUMBER: 91
POSITION: Center
SHOOTS: Right
HEIGHT: 6'1"
WEIGHT: 188 pounds
BIRTHDATE: February 7, 1990
BIRTHPLACE: Markham, Ontario, Canada
DRAFTED: 2008 / Tampa Bay (1st round / 1st overall)

Playing his first year of junior hockey with the Sarnia Sting, **STEVEN STAMKOS** reached ninety-two points in just sixty-three games. In his second season, he became the number-one-ranked player for the 2008 **NHL Entry Draft** by scoring 105 points. Tampa Bay selected him **first overall**, and in his NHL **rookie** season Stamkos scored twenty-three goals and recorded twenty-two assists. In his breakout second season, he and Sidney Crosby shared the Maurice Richard Trophy for scoring the **NHL**'s most goals, with fifty-one.

Stamkos is a good skater who can blast off quickly. He can **deke** very well, and he has an incredibly accurate shot. He plays with a good attitude and **work ethic** and is known for winning **face-offs**. He is a disciplined player who won't take a bad penalty.

MARTIN ST. LOUIS

TAMPA BAY LIGHTNING

NUMBER: 26
POSITION: Right wing / Left wing
SHOOTS: Left
HEIGHT: 5'8"
WEIGHT: 176 pounds
BIRTHDATE: June 18, 1975
BIRTHPLACE: Laval, Quebec, Canada
SIGNED AS FREE AGENT: 1998 / Calgary

MARTIN ST. LOUIS passed up a chance to play in the **QMJHL**, choosing instead to attend the University of Vermont where he was a star player for their hockey team. Ignoring his performance and rather concerned with his small size for a hockey player, no **NHL** team drafted him in his eligible draft year. That didn't stop St. Louis who, after setting a school record for points, entered the **NHL** as a **free agent** and quickly became one of the league's most consistent and skilled players. In 2003–04, Martin led the **NHL** in scoring and received the **Hart Memorial Trophy** as the **NHL**'s most valuable player. He was also presented with the **Lester B. Pearson Award** as the players' choice for MVP and helped the Tampa Bay Lightning win the **Stanley Cup.**

St. Louis can steer the puck up the ice and around defenders so well, you would think the puck was glued to his stick! He is a great team player who enjoys earning assists as much as scoring goals.

JOHN TAVARES

NEW YORK ISLANDERS

NUMBER: 91
POSITION: Center
SHOOTS: Left
HEIGHT: 6'0"
WEIGHT: 206 pounds
BIRTHDATE: September 20, 1990
BIRTHPLACE: Mississauga, Ontario, Canada
DRAFTED: 2009 / New York Islanders (1st round / 1st overall)

JOHN TAVARES was the CHL Player of the Year in 2007. He finished the season with seventy-two goals and 134 points—and he was still just sixteen years old! His impressive hockey skills made him the top-rated player for the 2009 **NHL Entry Draft,** and the New York Islanders enthusiastically selected him **first overall.**

This Canadian-born player is known as one of the hardest-working forwards in the **NHL.** He plays every shift with determination and amazing effort and **plays hard to the whistle** every time. He uses his strong **passing** skills to set up his linemates, is a forceful player in the corners, and battles for the puck **along the boards.** He holds his position in front of the net well and scores many goals with his quick **wrist shot.** He has solid leadership skills and tremendous on-ice confidence.

JOE THORNTON

SAN JOSE SHARKS

NUMBER: 19
POSITION: Center
SHOOTS: Left
HEIGHT: 6'4"
WEIGHT: 230 pounds
BIRTHDATE: July 2, 1979
BIRTHPLACE: London, Ontario, Canada
DRAFTED: 1997 / Boston (1st round / 1st overall)

As a **rookie** with the Sault Ste. Marie Greyhounds of the **OHL**, **JOE THORNTON** scored thirty goals and seventy-six points and was named the **OHL** and **CHL** Rookie of the Year. Thornton was ranked the top **prospect** for the 1997 **NHL Entry Draft,** and the Bruins picked him **first overall**. He played for Boston until the midpoint of the 2005 season, when he was **traded** to the Sharks. He has played in six **NHL All-Star Games** and won a gold medal playing for Canada at the 2010 Winter Olympics.

Thornton is a big and powerful **centerman** who will battle for the puck **along the boards.** He can fire quick, straight passes to his teammates and he assists on many goals—a league-leading ninety-six in 2006–07. He can control the puck well, has a booming **slap shot,** and can score at important times in a game. Thornton is well-liked and respected around the **NHL** for his hardworking style of hockey and his commitment to his team and respect for fans.

JONATHAN TOEWS

CHICAGO BLACKHAWKS

NUMBER: 19
POSITION: Center
SHOOTS: Left
HEIGHT: 6'2"
WEIGHT: 210 pounds
BIRTHDATE: April 29, 1988
BIRTHPLACE: Winnipeg, Manitoba, Canada
DRAFTED: 2006 / Chicago (1st round / 3rd overall)

JONATHAN TOEWS had an amazing 2010. He began the year winning Olympic Gold playing for his native Canada and was named to the tournament all-star team. Later that same spring, he won the **Stanley Cup** as the captain of the Blackhawks and was the series **MVP**. Toews is a member of the Triple Gold Club, an elite group of **NHL** players who have won the **Stanley Cup**, Olympic Gold, and a World Championship. Incredibly, only twenty-five players in the world have ever won all three. That's amazing!

Toews is one of the best players in today's game. He displays amazing confidence each time he steps on the ice. He is a tremendous leader and has impressive puck-handling skills. Toews **sees the ice well** and is an extremely creative playmaker. He has a great shot, can **deke**, and is great in shootouts.

GLOSSARY OF HOCKEY TERMS

AHL: American Hockey League

along the boards: area of ice next to the boards

alternate captain/assistant captain: player who helps the captain to lead the team

Art Ross Trophy: award presented to the NHL's leading scorer at the end of the season

back-check: a forward player skating back into his end to help on defense

Calder Memorial Trophy: award presented to the NHL Rookie of the Year

center/centerman: player who takes the middle position on the forward line and takes face-offs

CHL: Canadian Hockey League

Conn Smythe Trophy: award presented to the most valuable player in the Stanley Cup playoffs

the Cup: nickname for Lord Stanley's Cup

deke: a move that fakes out a goalie or defender

face-off: beginning of play; a referee or linesman drops the puck between two opposing players

first overall: player chosen in the NHL Entry Draft ahead of all others; usually, the player thought to be the best among those available

Frank J. Selke Trophy: award presented to the forward who helps most on defense

Guy Lafleur Trophy: award presented to the MVP of the QMJHL playoffs

Hart Memorial Trophy: award presented by the NHL to its most valuable player

hat trick: scoring three goals in the same game

IIHF: International Ice Hockey Federation

IIHF World Championship: annual hockey tournament where member countries of the IIHF compete

IIHF World Junior Championship: annual international hockey tournament between member countries of the IIHF, at which all competing players are under the age of twenty

Lady Byng Memorial Trophy: award presented to the NHL's most sportsmanlike player

Lester B. Pearson Award: trophy presented by the NHLPA to the player its members judge to be the most valuable in the regular season (now known as the Ted Lindsay Award)

lineup: group of players on a team taking part in the game

Lord Stanley's Cup: trophy presented to the NHL's championship team; originally named the Dominion Hockey Challenge Cup

MVP: most valuable player

NHL: National Hockey League

NHL All-Star Game: annual game in which the NHL's best players are invited to compete

NHL Entry Draft: annual event at which each NHL team chooses players aged eighteen and up who do not already belong to an NHL club

OHL: Ontario Hockey League

one-timer: puck shot by a player the instant after he receives a pass

on-ice awareness: knowing what is going on and where to stand to get the puck

opponent: opposing team, or a player from that team

pass: moving the puck to another player on the same team

play hard to the whistle: continuing to work hard on the ice until the referee blows the whistle to call for a stoppage in play

playmaker: player who can create scoring chances for his team

plus/minus rating: difference between the number of goals scored by and against your team while you are on the ice and the teams are at even strength

power play: situation in which one team has more players on the ice than their opponent, because the opponent has one or more players in the penalty box

prospect: junior hockey player under consideration by NHL teams

puck control: ability to keep the puck on your stick

QMJHL: Quebec Major Junior Hockey League

referee/linesman: on-ice officials who make sure the players follow the rules during the game

rookie: player in his first NHL season

roster: group of players on a team

see the ice: to know where other players and the puck are, and how plays are developing, at all times

set-up man: player who passes the puck well and helps his linemates score

slap shot: hard shot, taken by swinging the stick back

the slot: area in front of the net

special teams: groups of players who go on the ice for the power play or to kill penalties

Stanley Cup: short for Lord Stanley's Cup

Ted Lindsay Award: trophy awarded to the NHL's most outstanding player as voted by the players (formerly the Lester B. Pearson Award)

trade: transfer of a player from one team to another, in exchange for another player, draft choices, or cash

training camp: series of practices held before the beginning of the NHL season that help determine which players will be part of the team

two-way player: player who helps his team on both offense and defense

veteran: player with many years of playing experience in the NHL

WHL: Western Hockey League

work ethic: belief in working very hard for your team

wrist shot: quick shot, taken by snapping one's wrists

Published in Canada by Tundra Books, a division of Random House of Canada Limited,
One Toronto Street, Suite 300, Toronto, Ontario M5C 2V6

Published in the United States by Tundra Books of Northern New York,
P.O. Box 1030, Plattsburgh, New York 12901

Library of Congress Control Number: 2012955579

Library and Archives Canada Cataloguing in Publication

We are the goal scorers : the top point leaders of the NHL / NHLPA.

ISBN 978-1-77049-461-9. – ISBN 978-1-77049-462-6 (EPUB)

1. Hockey players—Biography—Juvenile literature.
2. National Hockey League—Juvenile literature. I. National Hockey League Players' Association

GV848.5.A1W425 2013   j796.962092'2   C2012-901290-4

We acknowledge the financial support of the Government of Canada through the Canada Book Fund and that of the Government of Ontario through the Ontario Media Development Corporation's Ontario Book Initiative. We further acknowledge the support of the Canada Council for the Arts and the Ontario Arts Council for our publishing program.

ONTARIO ARTS COUNCIL
CONSEIL DES ARTS DE L'ONTARIO

Photo credits: Sidney Crosby (Bruce Bennett/Getty), Pavel Datsyuk (Dave Reginek/Getty), Jordan Eberle (Gregory Shamus/Getty), Patrik Elias (Paul Bereswill/Getty), Marian Gaborik (Jamie Sabau/Getty), Claude Giroux (Abelimages/Getty), Marian Hossa (Jonathan Daniel/Getty), Jarome Iginla (Dave Sandford/Getty), Erik Karlsson (Bruce Bennett/Getty), Phil Kessel (Claus Andersen/Getty), Anze Kopitar (Don Smith/Getty), Ilya Kovalchuk (Harry How/Getty), Joffrey Lupul (Dale MacMillan/Getty), Evgeni Malkin (Len Redkoles/Getty), Rick Nash (Elsa/Getty), James Neal (Claus Andersen/Getty), Alex Ovechkin (Paul Bereswill/Getty), Zach Parise (Derek Leung/Getty), Daniel Sedin (Hannah Foslien/Getty), Henrik Sedin (Derek Leung/Getty), Tyler Seguin (Dave Sandford/Getty), Teemu Selanne (Jeff Gross/Getty), Jason Spezza (Bruce Bennett/Getty), Steven Stamkos (Claus Andersen/Getty), Martin St. Louis (Paul Bereswill/Getty), John Tavares (Alex Trautwig/Getty), Joe Thornton (Victor Decolongon/Getty), Jonathan Toews (Bill Smith/Getty)

Edited by Dorothy Milne
Designed by Leah Springate

www.tundrabooks.com

Printed and bound in Canada

1 2 3 4 5 6   18 17 16 15 14 13